Contents

Preface to the Old Testament Notes

1. ABOUT ten years ago I was prevailed upon to publish Explanatory Notes upon the New Testament. When that work was begun, and indeed when it was finished, I had no design to attempt any thing farther of the kind. Nay, I had a full determination, Not to do it, being throughly fatigued with the immense labour (had it been only this; tho' this indeed was but a small part of it,) of writing twice over a Quarto book containing seven or eight hundred pages.

2. But this was scarce published before I was importuned to write Explanatory Notes upon the Old Testament. This importunity I have withstood for many years. Over and above the deep conviction I had, of my insufficiency for such a work, of my want of learning, of understanding, of spiritual experience, for an undertaking more difficult by many degrees, than even writing on the New Testament, I objected, That there were many passages in the Old, which I did not understand myself, and consequently could not explain to others, either to their satisfaction, or my own. Above all, I objected the want of time: Not only as I have a thousand other employments, but as my Day is near spent, as I am declined into the vale of years. And to this day it appears to me as a dream, a thing almost incredible, that I should be entering upon a work of this kind, when I am entering into the sixty - third year of my age.

3. Indeed these considerations, the last particular, still appear to me of such weight, that I cannot entertain a thought of composing a body of Notes on the whole Old Testament. All the question remaining was, "Is there extant any Exposition which is worth abridging" Abundantly less time will suffice for this and less abilities of every kind. In considering this question, I soon turned my thought on the well - known Mr. Henry. He is allowed by all competent judges, to have been a person of strong understanding, of various learning, of solid

piety, and much experience in the ways of God. And his exposition is generally clear and intelligible, the thoughts being expressed in plain words: It is also found, agreeable to the tenor of scripture, and to the analogy of faith. It is frequently full, giving a sufficient explication of the passages which require explaining. It is in many parts deep, penetrating farther into the inspired writings than most other comments do. It does not entertain us with vain speculations, but is practical throughout: and usually spiritual too teaching us how to worship God, not in form only, but in spirit and in truth.

4. But it may be reasonably enquired, "If Mr. Henry's exposition be not only plain, sound, full, and deep, but practical, yea and spiritual too, what need is there of any other Or how is it possible to mend This to alter it for the better" I answer, very many who have This, have no need of any other: particularly those who believe (what runs thro' the whole work and will much recommend it to them) the doctrine of absolution, irrespective, unconditional Predestination. I do not advise these, much to trouble themselves about any other exposition than Mr. Henry's: this is sufficient, thro' the assistance of the Blessed Spirit, to make private Christians wise unto salvation, and (the Lord applying his word) throughly furnished unto every good work.

5. But then it is manifest on the other hand, every one cannot have this exposition. It is too large a purchase: there are thousands who would rejoice to have it; but it bears too high a price. They have not Six Guineas (the London price) in the world, perhaps from one year's end to another. And if they sometimes have, yet they have it not to spare; they need it for other occasions. How much soever therefore they desire so valuable a work, they must content themselves to go without it.

6. But suppose they have money enough to purchase, yet they

have not time enough to read it: the size is as unsurmountable an objection as the price itself. It is not possible for men who have their daily bread to earn by the sweat of their brows, who generally are confined to their work, from six in the morning 'till six in the evening, to find leisure for reading over six folios, each containing seven or eight hundred pages. These therefore have need of some other exposition than Mr. Henry's. As excellent as it is in its kind, it is not for their purpose; seeing they have neither money to make the purchase, nor time to read it over.

7. It is very possible then to mend this work valuable as it is, at least by shortening it. As the grand objection to it is the size, that objection may be removed: and they who at present have no possibility of profiting by it, while it is of so great a bulk and so high a price, may then enjoy part at least of the same advantage with those who have more money and more leisure. Few I presume that have the whole and leisure to read it, will concern themselves with an extract. But those who cannot have all, will (for the present at least) be glad to have a part. And they who complain it is too short, may yet serve themselves of it, 'till they can procure the long work.

8. But I apprehend this valuable work may be made more valuable still, by making it plainer as well as shorter. Accordingly what is here extracted from it, (which indeed makes but a small part of the following volumes) is considerably plainer than the original. In order to this not only all the Latin sentences occasionally interspersed are omitted, but whatever phrases or words are not so intelligible to persons of no education. Those only who frequently and familiarly converse with men that are wholly uneducated, can conceive how many expressions are mere Greek to them, which are quite natural to those who have any share of learning. It is not by reading, much less by musing alone, that we are enabled to suit our discourse to common capacities. It is only by actually talking with the vulgar, that we learn to

talk in a manner they can understand. And unless we do this, what do we profit them Do we not lose all our labour Should we speak as angels, we should be of no more use to them, than sounding brass or a tinkling cymbal.

9. Nay I apprehend what is extracted from Mr. Henry's work, may in some sense be more sound than the original. Understand me right: I mean more conformable to that glorious declaration, God willeth all men to be saved, and to come to the knowledge of his truth. And let it not be objected, That the making any alteration with regard to a point of doctrine, is a misrepresentation of the author's sense, and consequently an injury done to him. It would so, is an alteration were made of his words, so as to make them bear a different meaning; or if any words were recited as His, which he did not write. But neither of these is the case. Nothing is recited here as written by him which he did not write. Neither is any construction put upon his words, different from his own. But what he wrote in favour of Particular Redemption, is totally left out. And of this I here give express notice to the reader once for all.

10. Again. It certainly possible that a work abundantly shorter than Mr. Henry's may nevertheless be considerably fuller, in some particulars. There are many words which he passes over without any explanation at all; as taking it for granted that the reader already knows the meaning of them. But this is a supposition not to be made; it is an entire mistake. For instance: What does a common man know of an Omer, or a Hin "Why Moses explains his own meaning: "An Omer is the tenth part of an Ephah." True; but what does the honest man know of an Ephah Just as much as of an Omer. I suppose that which led Mr. Henry into these omissions, which otherwise are unaccountable, was the desire of not saying what others had said before, Mr. Pool in particular. This is easily gathered from his own words, "Mr. Pool's English Annotations are of admirable use; especially for "the explaining of scripture

phrases, opening the sense and clearing "of difficulties. I have industriously declined as much as I could what "is to be found there." I wish he had not. Or at least that he had given us the same sense in other words. Indeed he adds, "Those "and other annotations are most easy to be consulted upon occasion." Yes by those that have them: but that is not the case with the generality of Mr. Henry's readers. And besides they may justly expect that so large a comment will leave them no occasion to consult others.

11. It is possible likewise to penetrate deeper into the meaning of some scriptures than Mr. Henry has done. Altho' in general he is far from being a superficial writer, yet he is not always the same. Indeed if he had, he must have been more than man, considering the vastness of his work. It was scarce possible for any human understanding, to furnish out such a number of folios, without sinking sometimes into trite reflections and observations, rather lively than deep. A stream that runs wide and covers a large tract of land, will be shallow in some places. If it had been confined within a moderate channel, it might have flowed deep all along.

12. Nay, it cannot be denied, that there may be an exposition of scripture more closely practical, than some parts of Mr. Henry's are, as well as more spiritual. Even his exposition of the twentieth chapter of Exodus, where one would naturally have expected to find a compleat scheme of Christian practice, does not answer that expectation. Nor do I remember that he has any where given us, a satisfactory account of Spiritual Religion, of the kingdom of God within us, the fruit of Christ dwelling and reigning in the heart. This I hoped to have found particularly in the exposition of our Lord's Sermon upon the mount. But I was quite disappointed of my hope. It was not by any means what I expected.

13. I do not therefore intend the following Notes for a bare abridgment of Mr. Henry's exposition. Far from it: I not only

omit much more than nineteen parts out of twenty of what he has written, but make many alterations and many additions, well nigh from the beginning to the end. In particular, I every where omit the far greater part of his inferences from and improvement of the chapter. They who think these the most valuable part of the work, may have recourse to the author himself. I likewise omit great part of almost every note, the sum of which is retained: as it seems to be his aim, to say as much, whereas it is mine to say as little as possible. And I omit abundance of quaint sayings and lively antitheses; as, "God feeds his birds. Shall he not feed his babes!" "Pharaoh's princes: his pimps rather." Indeed every thing of this kind which occurred I have left quite untouched: altho' I am sensible these are the very flowers which numberless readers admire; nay which many, I doubt not, apprehend to be the chief beauties of the book. For that very reason I cannot but wish, they had never had a place therein; for this is a blemish, which is exceeding catching: he that admires it, will quickly imitate it. I used once to wonder, whence some whom I greatly esteem, had so many pretty turns in preaching. But when I read Mr. Henry, my wonder ceased. I saw, they were only copying after him: altho' many of them probably without designing or even adverting to it. They generally consulted his exposition of their text, and frequently just before preaching. And hence little witticisms and a kind of archness insensibly stole upon them, and took place of that strong, manly eloquence, which they would otherwise have learned from the inspired writers.

14. With regard to alterations, in what I take from Mr. Henry, I continually alter hard words into easy, and long sentences into short. But I do not knowingly alter the sense of any thing I extract from him, I only endeavour in several places, to make it more clear and determinate. I have here and there taken the liberty of altering a word in the text. But this I have done very sparingly, being afraid of venturing too far; as being conscious of my very imperfect acquaintance with the

Hebrew tongue. I have added very largely from Mr. Pool, as much as seemed necessary for common readers, in order to their understanding those words or passages, which Mr. Henry does not explain. Nay, from the time that I had more maturely considered Mr. Pool's annotations on the Bible, (which was soon after I had gone thro' the book of Genesis) I have extracted far more from him than from Mr. Henry: it having been my constant method, after reading the text, first to read and weigh what Mr. Pool observed upon every verse, and afterwards to consult Mr. Henry's exposition of the whole paragraph. In consequence of this, instead of short additions from Mr. Pool to supply what was wanting in Mr. Henry, (which was my first design) I now only make extracts from Mr. Henry, to supply so far as they are capable, what was wanting in Mr. Pool. I say, so far as they are capable: for I still found in needful to add to both such farther observations, as have from time to time occurred to my own mind in reading or thinking on the scriptures, together with such as I have occasionally extracted from other authors.

15. Every thinking man will now easily discern my design in the following sheets. It is not, to write sermons, essays or set discourses, upon any part of scripture. It is not to draw inferences from the text, or to shew what doctrines may be proved thereby. It is this: To give the direct, literal meaning, of every verse, of every sentence, and as far as I am able, of every word in the oracles of God. I design only, like the hand of a dial, to point every man to This: not to take up his mind with something else, how excellent soever: but to keep his eye fixt upon the naked Bible, that he may read and hear it with understanding. I say again, (and desire it may be well observed, that none may expect what they will not find) It is not my design to write a book, which a man may read separate from the Bible: but barely to assist those who fear God, in hearing and reading the bible itself, by shewing the natural sense of every part, in as few and plain words as I can.

16. And I am not without hopes, that the following notes may in some measure answer this end, not barely to unlettered and ignorant men, but also to men of education and, learning: (altho' it is true, neither these nor the Notes on the New Testament were principally designed for Them.) Sure I am, that tracts wrote in the most plain and simple manner, are of infinitely more service to me, than those which are elaborated with the utmost skill, and set off with the greatest pomp of erudition.

17. But it is no part of my design, to save either learned or unlearned men from the trouble of thinking. If so, I might perhaps write Folios too, which usually overlay, rather than help the thought. On the contrary, my intention is, to make them think, and assist them in thinking. This is the way to understand the things of God; Meditate thereon day and night; So shall you attain the best knowledge; even to know the only true God and Jesus Christ whom He hath sent. And this knowledge will lead you, to love Him, because he hath first loved us: yea, to love the Lord your God with all your heart, and with all your soul, and with all your mind, and with all your strength. Will there not then be all that mind in you, which was also in Christ Jesus And in consequence of this, while you joyfully experience all the holy tempers described in this book, you will likewise be outwardly holy as He that hath called you is holy, in all manner of conversation.

18. If you desire to read the scripture in such a manner as may most effectually answer this end, would it not be advisable, 1. To set apart a little time, if you can, every morning and evening for that purpose 2. At each time if you have leisure, to read a chapter out of the Old, and one out of the New Testament: is you cannot do this, to take a single chapter, or a part of one 3. To read this with a single eye, to know the whole will of God, and a fixt resolution to do it In order to know his will, you should, 4. Have a constant eye to

the analogy of faith; the connexion and harmony there is between those grand, fundamental doctrines, Original Sin, Justification by Faith, the New Birth, Inward and Outward Holiness. 5. Serious and earnest prayer should be constantly used, before we consult the oracles of God, seeing "scripture can only be understood thro' the same Spirit whereby "it was given." Our reading should likewise be closed with prayer, that what we read may be written on our hearts. 6. It might also be of use, if while we read, we were frequently to pause, and examine ourselves by what we read, both with regard to our hearts, and lives. This would furnish us with matter of praise, where we found God had enabled us to conform to his blessed will, and matter of humiliation and prayer, where we were conscious of having fallen short. And whatever light you then receive, should be used to the uttermost, and that immediately. Let there be no delay. Whatever you resolve, begin to execute the first moment you can. So shall you find this word to be indeed the power of God unto present and eternal salvation.

EDINBURGH,

April 25, 1765.

Introduction to Jonah

Probably Jonah himself was the penman of this book. In 2 Kings 14:25, we find, that he was of Gath - hepher in Galilee, a city that belongs to the tribe of Zebulon. We find also, that he was a messenger of mercy to Israel in the reign of Jeroboam the second. We have here a remarkable instance of God's mercy, toward repenting inners. And in Jonah we have a most remarkable type, of our Lord's burial and resurrection.

Chapter One

Jonah disobeys the command of God, ver. 1 - 3.
Is arrested by a storm, ver. 4 - 6.
Discovered to be the cause of the storm, ver. 7 - 10.
Cast into the sea and swallowed by a fish, ver. 11 - 17.

Verse 2

2 Arise, go to Nineveh, that great city, and cry against it; for their wickedness is come up before me.

That great city — It is said to have been one hundred and fifty furlongs in length, that is eighteen miles and three quarters, and eleven miles and one quarter in breadth.

Verse 3

3 But Jonah rose up to flee unto Tarshish from the presence of the LORD, and went down to Joppa; and he found a ship going to Tarshish: so he paid the fare thereof, and went down into it, to go with them unto Tarshish from the presence of the LORD.

From the presence — From the place where God usually had shewed himself present, by revealing his word and will to his prophets. Perhaps he might think God would not put him upon this work, when he was got into a strange country.

Verse 5

5 Then the mariners were afraid, and cried every man unto his god, and cast forth the wares that were in the ship into the sea, to lighten it of them. But Jonah was gone down into the sides of the ship; and he lay, and was fast asleep.

Into the sides — In some cabin or other, whither he went

before the storm arose.

Verse 6

6 So the shipmaster came to him, and said unto him, What meanest thou, O sleeper? arise, call upon thy God, if so be that God will think upon us, that we perish not.

Will think upon us — With pity and favour.

Verse 7

7 And they said every one to his fellow, Come, and let us cast lots, that we may know for whose cause this evil is upon us. So they cast lots, and the lot fell upon Jonah.

Cast lots — "Lots are an appeal to heaven in doubtful cases, and therefore not to be used but where the matter is undeterminable in any other way."

Verse 8

8 Then said they unto him, Tell us, we pray thee, for whose cause this evil is upon us; What is thine occupation? and whence comest thou? what is thy country? and of what people art thou?

Tell us — What hast thou done, for which God is so angry with thee, and with us for thy sake?

Verse 9

9 And he said unto them, I am an Hebrew; and I fear the LORD, the God of heaven, which hath made the sea and the dry land.

I fear — I worship and serve the true God; the eternal and

almighty God, who made and ruleth the heavens.

Verse 13

13 Nevertheless the men rowed hard to bring it to the land; but they could not: for the sea wrought, and was tempestuous against them.

Rowed hard — They were willing to be at any labour to save him.

Verse 14

14 Wherefore they cried unto the LORD, and said, We beseech thee, O LORD, we beseech thee, let us not perish for this man's life, and lay not upon us innocent blood: for thou, O LORD, hast done as it pleased thee.

Unto the Lord — Now they all cry to Jonah's God, to Jehovah.

And said — Let us not perish for taking away his life.

Hast done — Sending the tempest, arresting the prophet by it, detecting him by lot, sentencing him by his own mouth, and confirming the condemning sentence by the continuance of the storm.

Verse 16

16 Then the men feared the LORD exceedingly, and offered a sacrifice unto the LORD, and made vows.

Feared the Lord — Perhaps as Jonah's casting over-board was a type of Christ's death, so the effect it had upon the mariners might be a type of the conversion of the Heathen from idols unto God.

Made vows — Probably they vowed, they would ever worship him whom Jonah preached, the Creator of heaven and earth.

Verse 17

17 Now the LORD had prepared a great fish to swallow up Jonah. And Jonah was in the belly of the fish three days and three nights.

A great fish — The Hebrew word is, numbered, has appointed him for Jonah's receiver and deliverer. God has the command of all his creatures, and can make any of them serve his designs of mercy to his people.

Chapter Two

Jonah's prayer and deliverance.

Verse 2

2 And said, I cried by reason of mine affliction unto the LORD, and he heard me; out of the belly of hell cried I, and thou heardest my voice.

Affliction — Straits with which he was encompassed, his body and mind being both shut up, the one by the monstrous dungeon of the fish's belly, and the other by the terrors of the Almighty.

Heardest my voice — Of which undoubtedly God gave him an assurance in his own soul.

Verse 4

4 Then I said, I am cast out of thy sight; yet I will look again toward thy holy temple.

I said — With myself, I thought in the midst of my fears and sufferings.

Cast out — Cut off from all hope of life, and as it were forgotten of God.

I will look — Toward heaven.

Verse 5

5 The waters compassed me about, even to the soul: the depth closed me round about, the weeds were wrapped about my head.

The weeds — It seems to mean, my case was as hopeless as that of a man wrapt about with weeds in the depth of the sea.

Verse 6

6 I went down to the bottoms of the mountains; the earth with her bars was about me for ever: yet hast thou brought up my life from corruption, O LORD my God.

I went down — The fish carried him down as deep in the sea as are the bottoms of the mountains.

With her bars — I seemed to be imprisoned where the bars that secured were as durable as the rocks, which they were made of.

Yet — By what was first my danger, thou hast wonderfully secured me.

From corruption — Or the pit, a description of the state of the dead.

O Lord — In the assurance of faith, he speaks of the thing as already done.

Verse 7

7 When my soul fainted within me I remembered the LORD: and my prayer came in unto thee, into thine holy temple.

Thine holy temple — Heaven, the temple of his glory, whence God gives the command for his delivery.

Verse 8

8 They that observe lying vanities forsake their own mercy.

They — Whoever they are that depend upon idols.

Mercy — The Lord, who is to all that depend upon him, the fountain of living waters; who is an eternal fountain of mercy, and flows freely to all that wait for him.

Verse 9

9 But I will sacrifice unto thee with the voice of thanksgiving; I will pay that that I have vowed. Salvation is of the LORD.

Vowed — Which probably was to go to Nineveh, and preach what God commanded him.

The Lord — He only can save.

Verse 10

10 And the LORD spake unto the fish, and it vomited out Jonah upon the dry land.

Spake — Though fishes understand not as man, yet they have ears to hear their Creator.

Chapter Three

Jonah's mission renewed and executed, ver. 1 - 4.
The humiliation and reformation of the Ninevites, ver. 5 - 9.
Their sentence revoked, ver. 10.

Verse 3

3 So Jonah arose, and went unto Nineveh, according to the word of the LORD. Now Nineveh was an exceeding great city of three days' journey.

Exceeding great — The greatest city of the known world at that day, it was then in its flourishing state greater than Babylon, whose compass was three hundred eighty-five furlongs, but Nineveh was in compass, four hundred and eighty. It is said, her walls were an hundred foot in height, her walls broad enough for three coaches to meet, and safely pass by each other; that it had fifteen hundred towers on its walls, each two hundred foot high, and one million, four hundred thousand men employed for eight years to build it.

Of three days journey — To walk round the walls, allowing twenty miles to each day's journey.

Verse 4

4 And Jonah began to enter into the city a day's journey, and he cried, and said, Yet forty days, and Nineveh shall be overthrown.

Shall be overthrown — The threat is express. But there was a reserve with God, on condition of repentance.

Verse 5

5 So the people of Nineveh believed God, and proclaimed a

fast, and put on sackcloth, from the greatest of them even to the least of them.

From the greatest — Great and small, rich and poor.

Verse 6

6 For word came unto the king of Nineveh, and he arose from his throne, and he laid his robe from him, and covered him with sackcloth, and sat in ashes.

The king — Probably Phul Belochus.

His robe — Put off his rich apparel.

Verse 7

7 And he caused it to be proclaimed and published through Nineveh by the decree of the king and his nobles, saying, Let neither man nor beast, herd nor flock, taste any thing: let them not feed, nor drink water:

Taste any thing — Man and beast are to forbear to eat and drink, that the fast might be most solemn, that the cry of man, seconded with the cry of hungry cattle, might enter the ears of God, who preserveth man and beast.

Verse 8

8 But let man and beast be covered with sackcloth, and cry mightily unto God: yea, let them turn every one from his evil way, and from the violence that is in their hands.

And beast — Their horses and camels, both which they adorned with rich and costly clothing, they must now in testimony of an hearty repentance, clothe with sackcloth; the clothing of beasts must witness for men.

The violence — Oppression and rapine.

In their hands — Which are practised by them.

Chapter Four

Jonah repines at God's mercy, ver. 1 - 3.
Is reproved, ver. 4.
His discontent at the withering of the gourd, ver. 5 - 9.
God improves it for his conviction, ver. 10, 11.

Verse 1

1 But it displeased Jonah exceedingly, and he was very angry.

It — The divine forbearance sparing Nineveh.

Verse 2

2 And he prayed unto the LORD, and said, I pray thee, O LORD, was not this my saying, when I was yet in my country? Therefore I fled before unto Tarshish: for I knew that thou art a gracious God, and merciful, slow to anger, and of great kindness, and repentest thee of the evil.

Was not this — Did I not think of this? That thy pardon would contradict my preaching.

Verse 3

3 Therefore now, O LORD, take, I beseech thee, my life from me; for it is better for me to die than to live.

Than to live — Disgraced and upbraided by hardened sinners, who will brand me for a liar.

Verse 5

5 So Jonah went out of the city, and sat on the east side of the city, and there made him a booth, and sat under it in the shadow, till he might see what would become of the city.

A booth — Some small and mean shed, probably of green boughs.

'Till he might see — It seems the forty days were not fully expired.

Verse 6

6 And the LORD God prepared a gourd, and made it to come up over Jonah, that it might be a shadow over his head, to deliver him from his grief. So Jonah was exceeding glad of the gourd.

Prepared — Commanded that in the place where Jonah's booth stood, this spreading plant should spring up to be a shade when the gathered boughs were withered.

To deliver — To give some ease to his mind.

Verse 7

7 But God prepared a worm when the morning rose the next day, and it smote the gourd that it withered.

Prepared — By the same power which caused the gourd suddenly to spring, and spread itself.

It smote — Which early next morning, bit the root, so that the whole gourd withered.

Verse 8

8 And it came to pass, when the sun did arise, that God prepared a vehement east wind; and the sun beat upon the head of Jonah, that he fainted, and wished in himself to die, and said, It is better for me to die than to live.

A east wind — A dry, scorching, blasting wind.

Fainted — Overcome by the heat.

Better to die — But Jonah must be wiser, and humbler, and more merciful too, e'er he die. Before God hath done with him, he will teach him to value his own life more, and to be more tender of the life of others.

Verse 9

9 And God said to Jonah, Doest thou well to be angry for the gourd? And he said, I do well to be angry, even unto death.

I do well to be angry — If in the violence of this passion I should die (as some have) yet were I not to blame. What a speech! Verily the law made nothing perfect!

Verse 10

10 Then said the LORD, Thou hast had pity on the gourd, for the which thou hast not laboured, neither madest it grow; which came up in a night, and perished in a night:

Laboured — Thou didst not set it.

Grow — Nor didst thou water or give growth to it.

Verse 11

11 And should not I spare Nineveh, that great city, wherein are more than sixscore thousand persons that cannot discern between their right hand and their left hand; and also much cattle?

I — The God of infinite compassions and goodness.

That great city — Wouldest thou have me less merciful to such a goodly city, than thou art to a weed? Who cannot discern - Here are more than six-score innocents who are infants.

Much cattle — Beside men, women and children who are in Nineveh, there are many other of my creatures that are not sinful, and my tender mercies are and shall be over all my works. If thou wouldest be their butcher, yet I will be their God. Go Jonah, rest thyself content and be thankful: that goodness, which spared Nineveh, hath spared thee in this thy inexcusable frowardness. I will be to repenting Nineveh what I am to thee, a God gracious and merciful, slow to anger, and of great kindness, and I will turn from the evil which thou and they deserve.

30407447R00015

Printed in Great Britain
by Amazon